HAL•LEONARD
ESSENTIAL SONGS

PIANO VOCAL GUITAR

The 1970s

ISBN 0-634-09102-6

HAL•LEONARD®
CORPORATION

7777 W. BLUEMOUND RD. P.O. BOX 13819 MILWAUKEE, WI 53213

Visit Hal Leonard Online at
www.halleonard.com

CONTENTS

PAGE	SONG TITLE	ARTIST	PEAK	YEAR
4	ABC	The Jackson 5	1	1970
8	Afternoon Delight	Starland Vocal Band	1	1976
18	The Air That I Breathe	The Hollies	6	1974
22	American Pie	Don McLean	1	1972
32	At Seventeen	Janis Ian	3	1975
36	Baby Come Back	Player	1	1978
13	Baby, I Love Your Way	Peter Frampton	12	1976
42	Bad Girls	Donna Summer	1	1979
46	Baker Street	Gerry Rafferty	2	1978
50	Band on the Run	Paul McCartney & Wings	1	1974
54	Best of My Love	The Eagles	1	1975
64	Billy, Don't Be a Hero	Bo Donaldson & The Heywoods	1	1974
59	Boogie Nights	Heatwave	2	1977
68	The Boys Are Back in Town	Thin Lizzy	12	1976
72	Brandy (You're a Fine Girl)	Looking Glass	1	1972
75	Car Wash	Rose Royce	1	1977
82	Clair	Gilbert O'Sullivan	2	1972
90	The Closer I Get to You	Roberta Flack & Donny Hathaway	2	1978
87	Come and Get It	Badfinger	7	1970
94	Come Sail Away	Styx	8	1977
100	Cracklin' Rosie	Neil Diamond	1	1970
105	Da Ya Think I'm Sexy	Rod Stewart	1	1979
110	Daniel	Elton John	2	1973
120	Disco Lady	Johnnie Taylor	1	1976
126	Do You Know Where You're Going To?	Diana Ross	1	1976
132	Don't Give Up on Us	David Soul	1	1977
115	Dreams	Fleetwood Mac	1	1977
138	Dust in the Wind	Kansas	6	1978
144	Everything Is Beautiful	Ray Stevens	1	1970
148	Fame	David Bowie	1	1975
153	Feelings (¿Dime?)	Morris Albert	6	1975
156	The First Cut Is the Deepest	Rod Stewart	2	1977
160	Fly Like an Eagle	Steve Miller Band	2	1977
166	Garden Party	Rick Nelson	6	1972
169	Gypsys, Tramps and Thieves	Cher	1	1970
172	Hey There Lonely Girl (Hey There Lonely Boy)	Eddie Holman	2	1970
175	(Hey, Won't You Play) Another Somebody Done Somebody Wrong Song	B.J. Thomas	1	1975
178	Honky Cat	Elton John	8	1972
187	How Can You Mend a Broken Heart	The Bee Gees	1	1971
190	How Long	ACE	3	1975
193	Hurting Each Other	Carpenters	2	1972
196	I Can Help	Billy Swan	1	1974
199	I Feel the Earth Move	Carole King	F	1971

206	(I Never Promised You A) Rose Garden	Lynn Anderson	1	1970
211	I Think I Love You	Partridge Family	1	1970
218	I Wish	Stevie Wonder	1	1977
228	I'll Take You There	The Staple Singers	1	1972
234	If	Bread	4	1971
223	If You Leave Me Now	Chicago	1	1976
238	It Never Rains (In Southern California)	Albert Hammond	5	1972
252	It's So Easy	Linda Ronstadt	5	1977
254	Jazzman	Carole King	2	1974
243	Just the Way You Are	Billy Joel	3	1978
258	Knock Three Times	Dawn	1	1971
261	Lay Down Sally	Eric Clapton	3	1978
264	Let It Be	The Beatles	1	1970
269	The Logical Song	Supertramp	6	1979
274	Looks Like We Made It	Barry Manilow	1	1977
277	Me and You and a Dog Named Boo	Lobo	5	1971
280	Morning Has Broken	Cat Stevens	6	1972
285	My Love	Paul McCartney & Wings	1	1973
288	Nothing from Nothing	Billy Preston	1	1974
293	Peg	Steely Dan	1	1978
296	Precious and Few	Climax	3	1972
300	Raindrops Keep Fallin' on My Head	B.J. Thomas	1	1970
303	A Rainy Night in Georgia	Brook Benton	4	1970
306	Rikki Don't Lose That Number	Steely Dan	4	1974
310	Sara Smile	Daryl Hall & John Oates	4	1976
313	Shambala	Three Dog Night	3	1973
318	Smoke on the Water	Deep Purple	4	1973
322	Stayin' Alive	The Bee Gees	1	1978
332	Summer Breeze	Seals & Crofts	6	1972
327	Superstition	Stevie Wonder	1	1973
338	Take a Chance on Me	ABBA	3	1978
344	Take Me Home, Country Roads	John Denver	2	1971
352	Three Times a Lady	Commodores	1	1978
358	Time in a Bottle	Jim Croce	1	1973
349	The Way We Were	Barbra Streisand	1	1974
362	We Are the Champions	Queen	4	1978
366	What's Going On	Marvin Gaye	2	1971
372	When I Need You	Leo Sayer	1	1977
378	Yesterday Once More	Carpenters	2	1973
375	You Are the Sunshine of My Life	Stevie Wonder	1	1973
382	You Light Up My Life	Debby Boone	1	1977
398	You're So Vain	Carly Simon	1	1973
386	You've Got a Friend	James Taylor	1	1971
392	Your Song	Elton John	8	1971

ABC

Words and Music by ALPHONSO MIZELL,
FREDERICK PERREN, DEKE RICHARDS and BERRY GORDY

With drive

Buh, buh, buh, buh, buh, boo, buh, buh, buh, buh, buh, buh. You

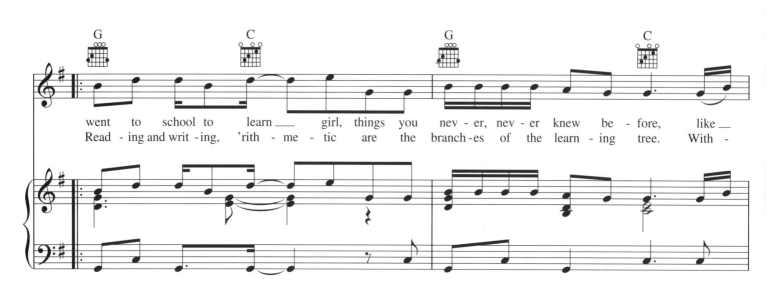

went to school to learn ___ girl, things you nev-er, nev-er knew be-fore, like
Read-ing and writ-ing, 'rith-me-tic are the branch-es of the learn-ing tree. With-

"I" be-fore "E" ex-cept af-ter "C" and why two plus two makes four. Now, now, now
out the roots of a love ev-'ry day, girl, your ed-u-ca-tion ain't com-plete.

Bass Vamp

AFTERNOON DELIGHT

Words and Music by
BILL DANOFF

BABY, I LOVE YOUR WAY

Words and Music by
PETER FRAMPTON

THE AIR THAT I BREATHE

Words and Music by ALBERT HAMMOND
and MICHAEL HAZELWOOD

AMERICAN PIE

Words and Music by
DON McLEAN

Additional Lyrics

2. Now for ten years we've been on our own,
   And moss grows fat on a rollin' stone
   But that's not how it used to be
   When the jester sang for the king and queen
   In a coat he borrowed from James Dean
   And a voice that came from you and me
   Oh and while the king was looking down,
   The jester stole his thorny crown
   The courtroom was adjourned,
   No verdict was returned
   And while Lenin read a book on Marx
   The quartet practiced in the park
   And we sang dirges in the dark
   The day the music died
   We were singin'...bye-bye... etc.

3. Helter-skelter in the summer swelter
   The birds flew off with a fallout shelter
   Eight miles high and fallin' fast,
   It landed foul on the grass
   The players tried for a forward pass,
   With the jester on the sidelines in a cast
   Now the half-time air was sweet perfume
   While the sergeants played a marching tune
   We all got up to dance
   But we never got the chance
   'Cause the players tried to take the field,
   The marching band refused to yield
   Do you recall what was revealed
   The day the music died
   We started singin'... bye-bye...etc.

4. And there we were all in one place,
   A generation lost in space
   With no time left to start again
   So come on, Jack be nimble, Jack be quick,
   Jack Flash sat on a candlestick
   'Cause fire is the devil's only friend
   And as I watched him on the stage
   My hands were clenched in fits of rage
   No angel born in hell
   Could break that Satan's spell
   And as the flames climbed high into the night
   To light the sacrificial rite
   I saw Satan laughing with delight
   The day the music died
   He was singin'...bye-bye...etc.

AT SEVENTEEN

Words and Music by
JANIS IAN

Moderately

Guitar (capo V) → G(add9) G Gmaj7 G6 G G(add9) G Gmaj7 G6 G

Keyboard → C(add9) C Cmaj7 C6 C C(add9) C Cmaj7 C6 C

I

G(add9) G Gmaj7 G6 G Am11 Am7 E/A
C(add9) C Cmaj7 C6 C Dm11 Dm7 A/D

learned the truth at sev - en - teen, ___ that love was meant for beau -
brown - eyed girl in hand - me - downs ___ whose name I nev - er could ___
those of us who know ___ the pain ___ of val - en - tines that nev -

Am7 D7
Dm7 G7

- ty queens ___ and high school girls ___ with clear - skinned smiles ___ who
___ pro - nounce ___ said, "Pit - y, please, ___ the ones ___ who serve. ___ They
- er came, ___ and those whose names ___ were nev - er called ___ when

BABY COME BACK

Words and Music by JOHN C. CROWLEY
and PETER BECKETT

BAD GIRLS

Words and Music by JOE "BEANS" ESPOSITO, EDWARD HOKENSON,
BRUCE SUDANO and DONNA SUMMER

BAKER STREET

Words and Music by
GERRY RAFFERTY

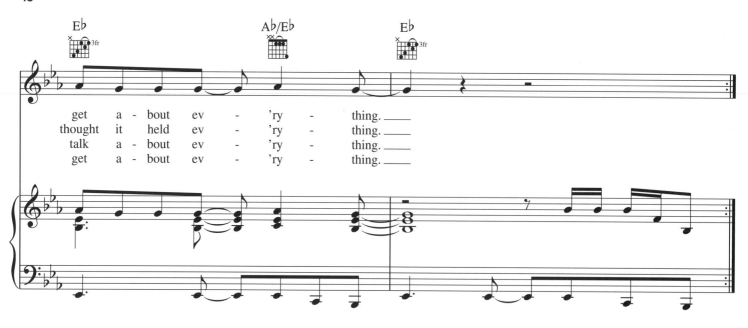

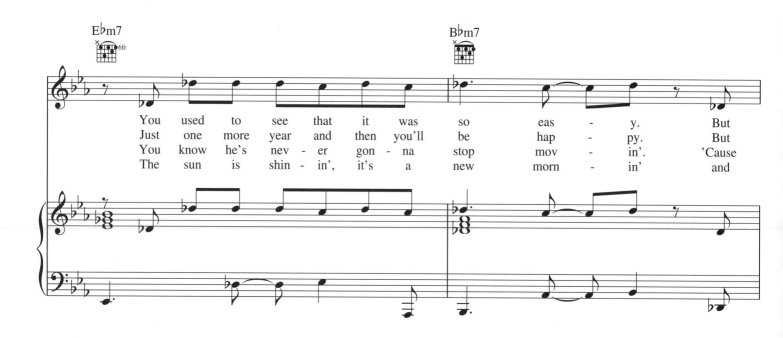

1, 3
Db
Ab
Eb
3fr
4fr
you're try - in', you're try - in' now.
you're cry - in', you're cry - in' now.
he's roll - in', he's the roll - in' stone.
you're go - in', you're go - in' home.
2, 4
Bb
Gb/Ab
Eb
Gb/Bb
6fr
Bbm
1
2
Ab7
1st time: D.S. (with repeats)
2nd time: Repeat and Fade
3

BAND ON THE RUN

Words and Music by
PAUL and LINDA McCARTNEY

Brighter beat

1. Well, the

rain ex- plod -ed with a might-y crash___ As we fell in -to___ the sun,___
un -der- tak -er drew a heav-y sigh___ See-ing no one else___ had come,___
night was fall -ing as the des-ert world___ Be- gan to set- tle down.___

And the first one said to the sec-ond one there___ I hope you're hav-ing fun.___
And a bell was ring-ing in the vil -lage square___ For the rab-bits on the run.___
In the town they're search-ing for us ev- 'ry where___ But we nev- er will be found.___

BEST OF MY LOVE

Words and Music by JOHN DAVID SOUTHER,
DON HENLEY and GLENN FREY

BOOGIE NIGHTS

Words and Music by
ROD TEMPERTON

BILLY, DON'T BE A HERO

Words and Music by PETER CALLENDER
and MITCH MURRAY

Bil - ly, don't be a he - ro, come back and make me your wife." _____

And as they start - ed to go _____ she said,

"Bil - ly, keep your head low. _____ Bil - ly, don't be a he - ro, come back to

me." _____

D.S. al Coda

CODA

I heard she threw that let - ter _____ a - way. _____

Repeat and Fade

THE BOYS ARE BACK IN TOWN

Words and Music by
PHILIP PARRIS LYNOTT

Moderately fast

1. Guess who just got back to day? Them wild - eyed boys
2.,3. *(See additional lyrics)*

that had been a - way. Had - n't changed, had - n't much to say,

but, man, I still think them cats are cra - zy. They were ask - ing if you

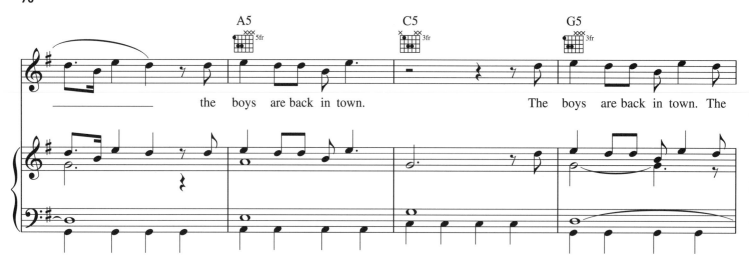

the boys are back in town. The boys are back in town. The

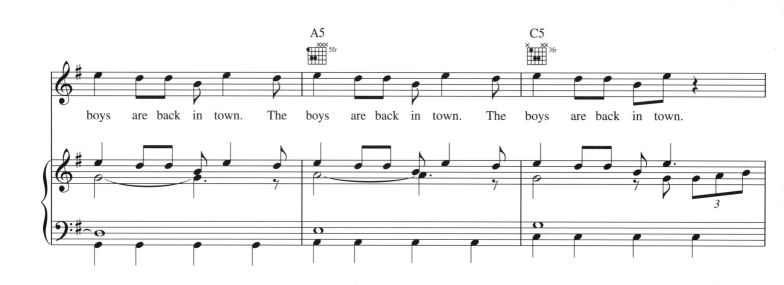

boys are back in town. The boys are back in town. The boys are back in town.

(Fade on D.S.)

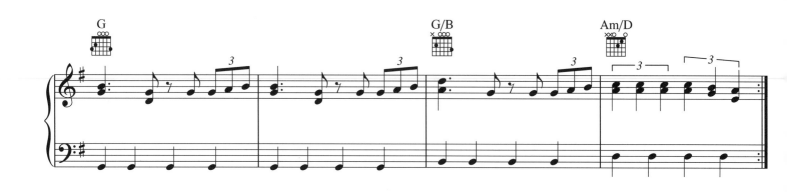

Interlude

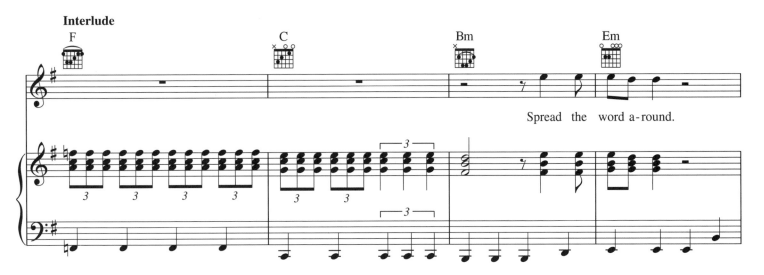

Spread the word a-round.

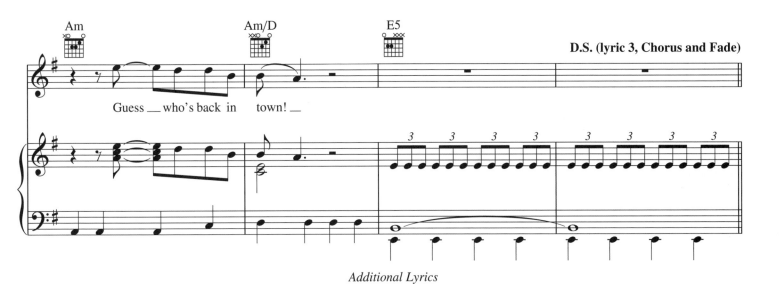

D.S. (lyric 3, Chorus and Fade)

Guess __ who's back in town! __

Additional Lyrics

2. You know that chick that used to dance a lot
   Every night she'd be on the floor shaking what she'd got
   Man, when I tell you she was cool, she was hot
   I mean she was steaming.

   And that time over at Johnny's place
   Well, this chick got up and she slapped Johnny's face
   Man, we just fell about the place
   If that chick don't wanna know, forget her.

   (Chorus & Interlude)

3. Friday night they'll be dressed to kill
   Down at Dino's Bar and Grill
   The drink will flow and blood will spill
   And if the boys want to fight, you better let 'em.

   That jukebox in the corner blasting out my favorite song
   The nights are getting warmer, it won't be long
   It won't be long till summer comes
   Now that the boys are here again.

   (Chorus and Fade)

BRANDY
(You're a Fine Girl)

Words and Music by
ELLIOT LURIE

CAR WASH

Words and Music by
NORMAN WHITFIELD

Moderately slow (with a double time feel)

Come on and sing it with me car wash. __

To Coda ⊕

Get with the feel - in' y'all __ car wash __ yeah.

N.C.

1

Come sum-mer the work gets kind-a hard. __

__ This ain't no place to be if ya

Repeat and Fade

CLAIR

Words and Music by
GILBERT O'SULLIVAN

COME AND GET IT

Words and Music by
PAUL McCARTNEY

Will you walk a - way from a fool and his mo — ney —— If you
want it, here — it is, Come and get it but you bet-ter hur -ry 'cos it's go-ing fast —
If you
Son - ny if you want it here — it is, Come and get it, but you bet-ter

To Coda

(tacet-------------)

D.%. al Coda

CODA

(tacet-------------)

2 The chord on beat 1 is E major.

THE CLOSER I GET TO YOU

Words and Music by JAMES MTUME
and REGGIE LUCAS

COME SAIL AWAY

Words and Music by
DENNIS DeYOUNG

Moderately slow, with feeling

CRACKLIN' ROSIE

Words and Music by
NEIL DIAMOND

Moderately fast

DA YA THINK I'M SEXY

Words and Music by ROD STEWART
and CARMINE APPICE

DANIEL

Words and Music by ELTON JOHN
and BERNIE TAUPIN

Moderately fast

(1.,4.) Dan - iel is trav -
(2.) They say Spain is pret -
(3.) *Instrumental ad lib.*

- 'ling to - night __ on a plane. __
- ty, __ 'though I've nev - er been. __

Oh God, _____ it looks like Dan - iel.

Must be _____ the clouds _____ in _____ my _____ eyes. _____

DREAMS

Words and Music by
STEVIE NICKS

DISCO LADY

Words and Music by DON DAVIS,
HARVEY SCALES and AL VANCE

Moderate Disco

Shake it up, shake it down; move it in, move it 'round, dis-co la-dy. ___ Move it in, move it out; move it in and a-bout, dis-co la-dy. ___ Shake it

DO YOU KNOW WHERE YOU'RE GOING TO?

Theme from MAHOGANY

Words by GERRY GOFFIN
Music by MIKE MASSER

DON'T GIVE UP ON US

Words and Music by
TONY MACAULAY

Moderately slow

1. Don't give

up on us ba - by, ___ don't make the wrong seem
(2., D.S.) up on us ba - by ___ we're still worth one more

right, the fu - ture is - n't just one ___ night, ___
try, and tho' we put a last one ___ by, ___

DUST IN THE WIND

Words and Music by
KERRY LIVGREN

Moderate Folk style

Ev - 'ry - thing __ is dust in the wind.

wind.)

Repeat and Fade

Optional Ending

poco rit.

EVERYTHING IS BEAUTIFUL

Words and Music by
RAY STEVENS

2. We shouldn't care about the length of his hair or the color of his skin,
   Don't worry about what shows from without but the love that lives within,
   We gonna get it all together now and everything gonna work out fine,
   Just take a little time to look on the good side my friend and straighten it out in your mind.

FAME

Words and Music by JOHN LENNON,
DAVID BOWIE and CARLOS ALOMAR

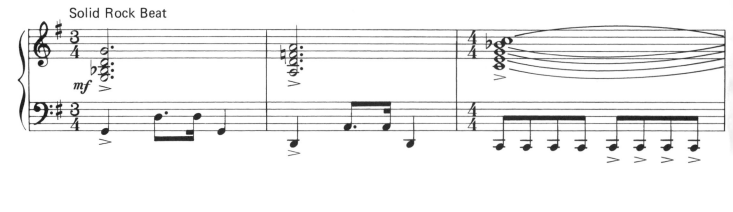

Solid Rock Beat

1. Fame____ makes a man____ take things o- ver.____ Fame____ lets him
2. Fame,____ what you like____ is in the li- mo.____ Fame,____ what you

loose, hard to swal- low.____ Fame____ puts you there____ where things are hol- low,____
get is no to-mor- row.____ Fame,____ what you need____ you have to bor- row,____

Fame, _____ fame, _____ fame, _____ fame, _____

fame, _____ fame, fame, fame, fame, fame, fame, fame, fame, fame, fame,

fame, fame, fame, Fame, _____ what's your name?

Repeat and Fade

FLY LIKE AN EAGLE

Words and Music by
STEVE MILLER

Moderately (not too fast)

Time flies, don't it, babe? __ Do do do do.

Do do do do. Do do do do. Do do do do.

I wan-na fly __

GARDEN PARTY

Words and Music by
RICK NELSON

Moderate Rock

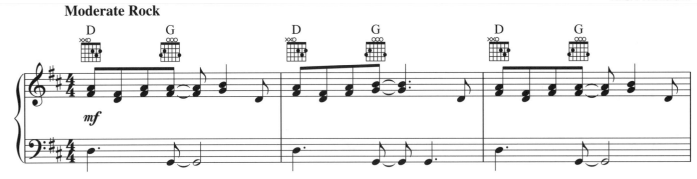

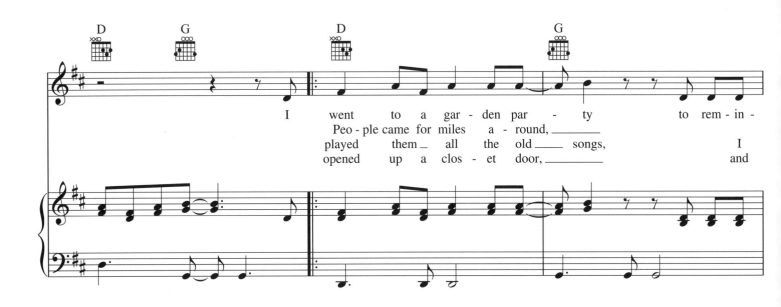

I went to a gar-den par-ty to rem-in-
Peo-ple came for miles a-round, _____
played them _____ all the old _____ songs, _____ I
opened up a clos-et door, _____ and

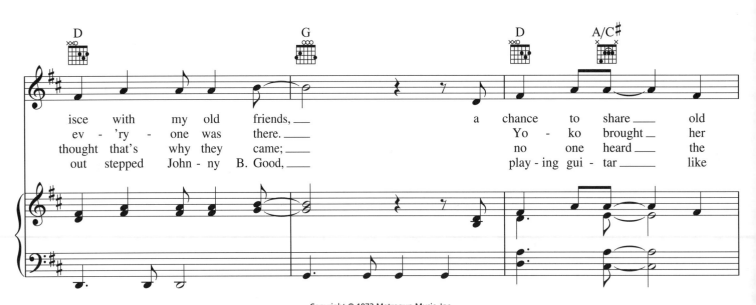

isce with my old friends, _____ a chance to share _____ old
ev-'ry-one was there. _____ Yo-ko brought _____ her
thought that's why they came; _____ no one heard _____ the
out stepped John-ny B. Good, _____ play-ing gui-tar _____ like

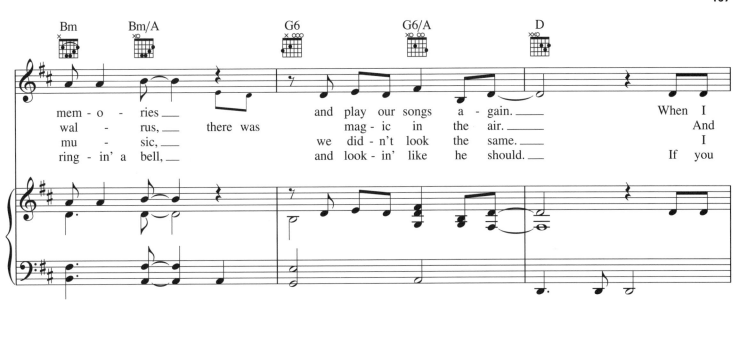

mem - o - ries ____ and play our songs a - gain. ____ When I
wal - rus, ____ there was mag - ic in the air. ____ And
mu - sic, ____ we did - n't look the same. ____ I
ring - in' a bell, ____ and look - in' like he should. ____ If you

got to the gar - den par - ty, they all knew __ my name, __
o - ver __ in the cor - ner, much to my __ sur - prise, __
said hel - lo to "Mar - y Lou," she be - longs __ to me. __
got - ta play at gar - den par - ties, I wish you a lot of luck, __

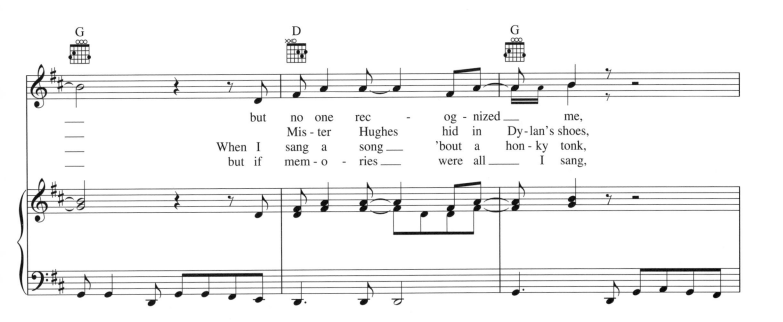

____ but no one rec - og - nized ____ me,
____ Mis - ter Hughes hid in Dy - lan's shoes,
____ When I sang a song ____ 'bout a hon - ky tonk,
____ but if mem - o - ries ____ were all ____ I sang,

GYPSYS, TRAMPS AND THIEVES

Words and Music by
ROBERT STONE

HEY THERE LONELY GIRL
(Hey There Lonely Boy)

Words and Music by EARL SHUMAN
and LEON CARR

(Hey, Won't You Play)
ANOTHER SOMEBODY DONE SOMEBODY WRONG SONG

Words and Music by LARRY BUTLER
and CHIPS MOMAN

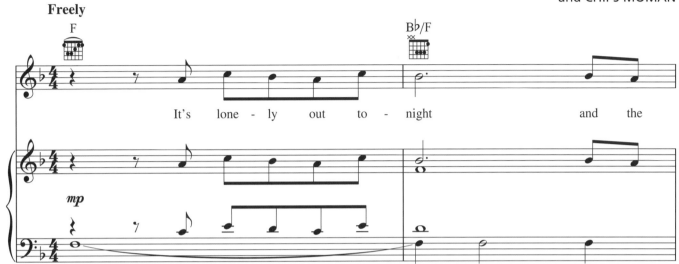

It's lone-ly out to-night and the

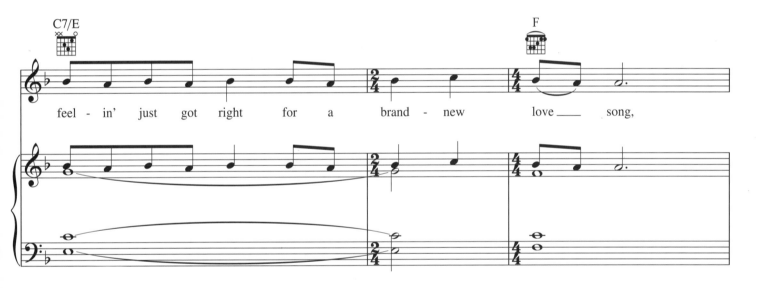

feel-in' just got right for a brand-new love___ song,

some-bod-y done some-bod-y wrong song.

HONKY CAT

Words and Music by ELTON JOHN
and BERNIE TAUPIN

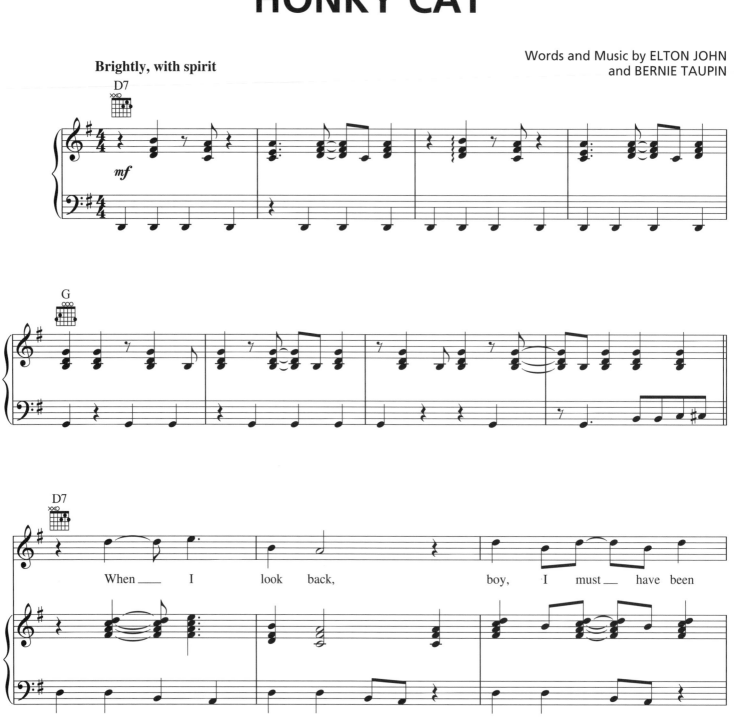

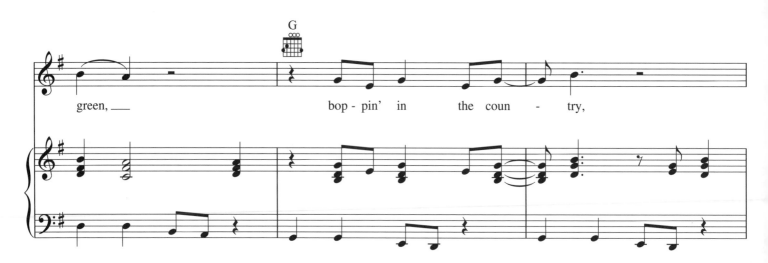

When ___ I look back, boy, I must ___ have been green, ___ bop-pin' in the coun-try,

HOW CAN YOU MEND
A BROKEN HEART

Words and Music by ROBIN GIBB
and BARRY GIBB

Slowly

I can think of young-er days when liv-ing for my life was
I can still feel the breeze that rus-tles through the trees and

ev-'ry-thing a man could want to do.
mist-y mem-o-ries of days gone by.

I could nev-er see to-
We could nev-er see to-

HOW LONG

Words and Music by
PAUL CARRACK

HURTING EACH OTHER

Words by PETER UDELL
Music by GARY GELD

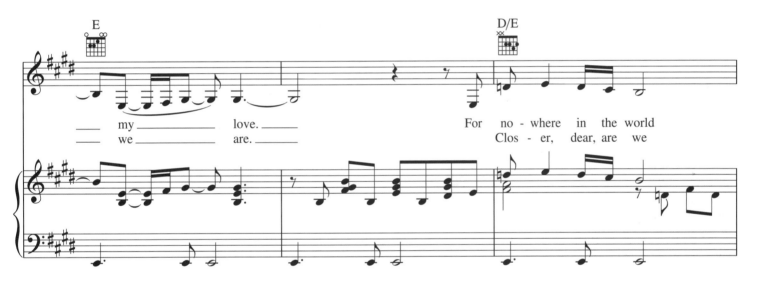

I CAN HELP

Words and Music by
BILLY SWAN

I FEEL THE EARTH MOVE

Words and Music by
CAROLE KING

The original recording contains two separate piano parts. For this arrangement, they have been combined to be playable as a solo.

(I Never Promised You A)
ROSE GARDEN

Words and Music by
JOE SOUTH

Moderately bright, with a beat

I beg your par - don, I nev - er prom - ised you a rose ___ gar - den.

A - long with the sun - shine, there's got to be a lit - tle rain ___ some - time.

When you take you got to give, so live and let live ___ or let

I THINK I LOVE YOU

Words and Music by
TONY ROMEO

wor-ries me to say___ that I'd nev - er felt___ this way.

I WISH

Words and Music by
STEVIE WONDER

IF YOU LEAVE ME NOW

Words and Music by
PETER CETERA

Ooh, _____ girl, _____ just
Ooh, ma - ma, _____ I just

got to have _ you by my side. _____
got to have _ your lov - in'. _____

Repeat and Fade

Ooh, _____

I'LL TAKE YOU THERE

Words and Music by
ALVERTIS ISBELL

I know a ___ place

ain't no-bod-y cry-in',

ain't no-bod-y

wor-ried,

ain't no smil-in' fac-es

IF

Words and Music by
DAVID GATES

IT NEVER RAINS
(In Southern California)

Words and Music by ALBERT HAMMOND
and MICHAEL HAZELWOOD

Got on board ___ a west ___ bound sev - en for - ty - sev -

- en, ___ did - n't think ___ be - fore ___ de - cid -

- ing what ___ to do. All that talk of op - por - tu -

JUST THE WAY YOU ARE

Words and Music by
BILLY JOEL

IT'S SO EASY

Words and Music by BUDDY HOLLY
and NORMAN PETTY

JAZZMAN

Words and Music by CAROLE KING
and DAVID PALMER

Lift me, won't you lift me a-bove the old rou-tine; Make it nice,_____ play it clean,_____ jazz-man._____

KNOCK THREE TIMES

Words and Music by IRWIN LEVINE
and L. RUSSELL BROWN

LAY DOWN SALLY

Words and Music by ERIC CLAPTON,
MARCY LEVY and GEORGE TERRY

LET IT BE

Words and Music by JOHN LENNON
and PAUL McCARTNEY

When I find my-self __ in times of trou-ble

Instrumental

Moth-er Mar-y comes to me speak-ing words of wis-dom; let it

be. __ And in my hour of dark-ness, she is

THE LOGICAL SONG

Words and Music by RICK DAVIES
and ROGER HODGSON

Moderate Rock

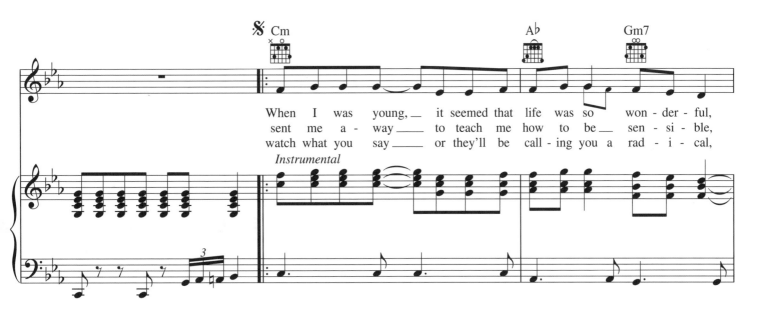

When I was young, __ it seemed that life was so won-der-ful,
sent me a-way __ to teach me how to be __ sen-si-ble,
watch what you say __ or they'll be call-ing you a rad-i-cal,

Instrumental

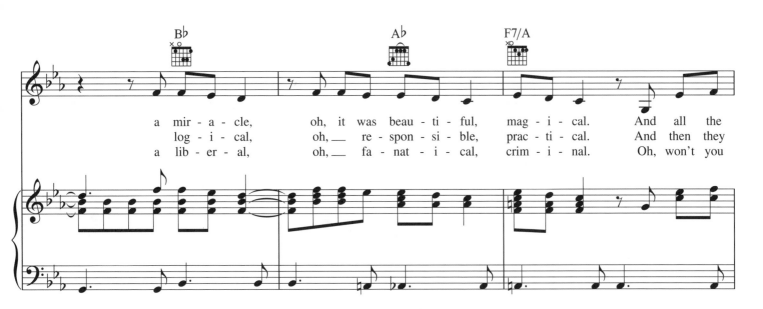

a mir-a-cle, oh, it was beau-ti-ful, mag-i-cal. And all the
log-i-cal, oh, __ re-spon-si-ble, prac-ti-cal. And then they
a lib-er-al, oh, __ fa-nat-i-cal, crim-i-nal. Oh, won't you

LOOKS LIKE WE MADE IT

Words and Music by RICHARD KERR
and WILL JENNINGS

1

Dm7   C/E   F   F/G   C(add9)   C   G/C   F/C

all I could taste was love __ the way we made it.

2

Dm7   C/E   F   G11   Am7

all I could taste was love __ the way we made __ it.

Em7   Am7   G11

Oh, we made it. Looks like we

C   Cmaj9   F/C

Repeat and Fade

made it. Looks like we

ME AND YOU AND A DOG NAMED BOO

Words and Music by
LOBO

MORNING HAS BROKEN

Musical Arrangement by CAT STEVENS
Words by ELEANOR FARJEON

282

MY LOVE

Words and Music by
PAUL and LINDA McCARTNEY

And when I go a - way_ I know my heart can stay_ with my
And when the cup - board's bare_ I'll still find some - thing there_ with my
Don't ev - er ask me why_ I nev - er say good-bye_ to my

love. It's un - der - stood_____ It's in the hands_ of my love, _____ and
love. It's un - der - stood_____ It's ev - 'ry-where_ with my love, _____
love. It's un - der - stood_____ It's ev - 'ry-where_ with my love, _____

my love does it good, Wo wo wo wo, wo wo

NOTHING FROM NOTHING

Words and Music by BILLY PRESTON
and BRUCE FISHER

Energetically, in 2

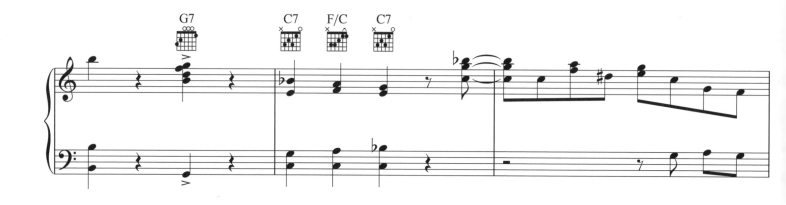

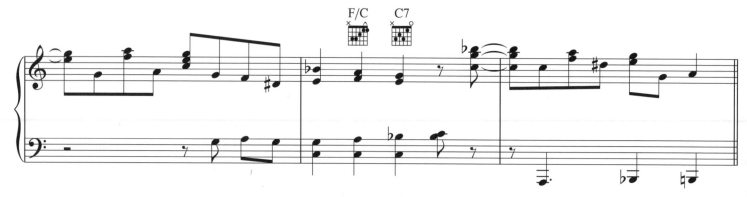

PEG

Words and Music by WALTER BECKER
and DONALD FAGEN

Moderately fast

I've seen your pic - ture, _
I like your pin shot. _

your name in lights a - bove it. _
I keep it with your let - ter. _

This is your
Done up in

PRECIOUS AND FEW

Words and Music by
WALTER D. NIMS

A RAINY NIGHT IN GEORGIA

Words and Music by
TONY JOE WHITE

D♭maj7   **E♭maj7**

it still comes out the same; no

Fm   **Gm**   **Fm**

mat- ter how you look at it, think of it, you

A♭   **Gm**   **Fm**   **E♭maj7**   **D♭maj7**

D.C. al Fine

just got to do ___ your own thing. ___

Additional Lyrics

3. I find me a place in a box car,
    So I take out my guitar to pass some time;
    Late at night when it's hard to rest,
    I hold your picture to my chest, and I'm all right.
    (To Chorus)

RIKKI DON'T LOSE THAT NUMBER

Words and Music by WALTER BECKER
and DONALD FAGEN

SARA SMILE

Words and Music by DARYL HALL
and JOHN OATES

SHAMBALA

Words and Music by
DANIEL MOORE

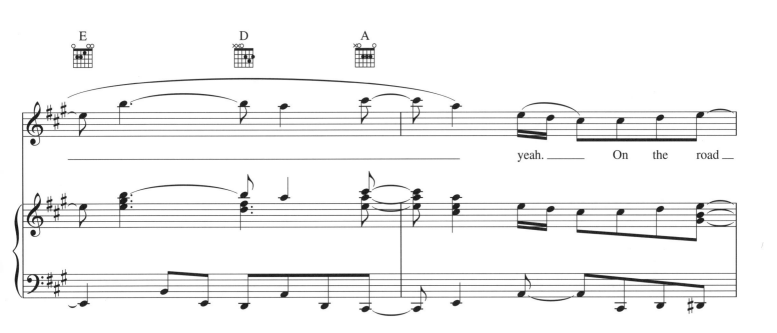

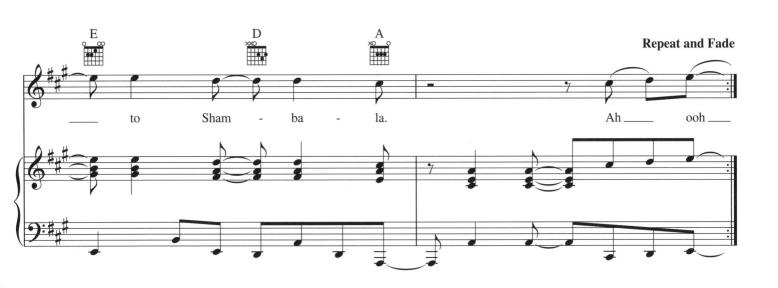

SMOKE ON THE WATER

Words and Music by RITCHIE BLACKMORE, IAN GILLAN,
ROGER GLOVER, JON LORD and IAN PAICE

We all came out to Mon-
They burned down the gam-
We end-ed up at the Grand

STAYIN' ALIVE
from the Motion Picture SATURDAY NIGHT FEVER

Words and Music by ROBIN GIBB,
MAURICE GIBB and BARRY GIBB

SUPERSTITION

Words and Music by
STEVIE WONDER

D.S. al Coda

Ver - y su - per - sti -

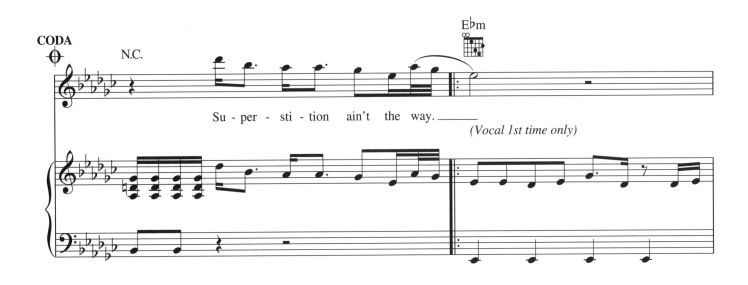

CODA

N.C.

E♭m

Su - per - sti - tion ain't the way._____

(Vocal 1st time only)

Repeat and Fade

Optional Ending

SUMMER BREEZE

Words and Music by JAMES SEALS
and DASH CROFTS

See the cur-tains hang - in' in the win-dow ___ in the eve-ning on a Fri-day night. ___
See the pa-per lay - in' on the side-walk, ___ a lit-tle mu - sic from the house next door. ___

A lit-tle light a shin - in' through the win - dow ___
So I walk on up to the door-step, ___

TAKE A CHANCE ON ME

Words and Music by BENNY ANDERSSON
and BJORN ULVAEUS

Moderate dance beat

If you change your mind ___ I'm the first in line.

___ Hon-ey, I'm still free, ___ take a chance on me. ___ If you need me let ___

___ me know, gon-na be a-round. ___ If you got no place ___

___ to go when you're feel-ing down. ___

TAKE ME HOME, COUNTRY ROADS

Words and Music by JOHN DENVER,
BILL DANOFF and TAFFY NIVERT

THE WAY WE WERE
from the Motion Picture THE WAY WE WERE

Words by ALAN and MARILYN BERGMAN
Music by MARVIN HAMLISCH

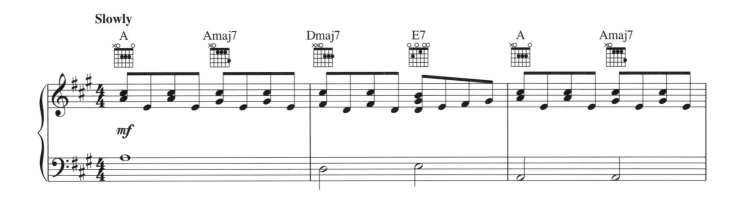

THREE TIMES A LADY

Words and Music by
LIONEL RICHIE

TIME IN A BOTTLE

Words and Music by
JIM CROCE

WE ARE THE CHAMPIONS

Words and Music by
FREDDIE MERCURY

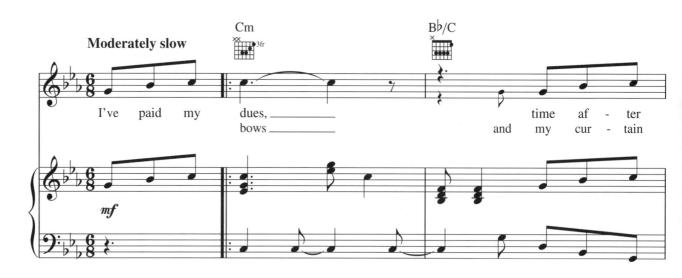

WHAT'S GOING ON

Words and Music by MARVIN GAYE,
AL CLEVELAND and RENALDO BENSON

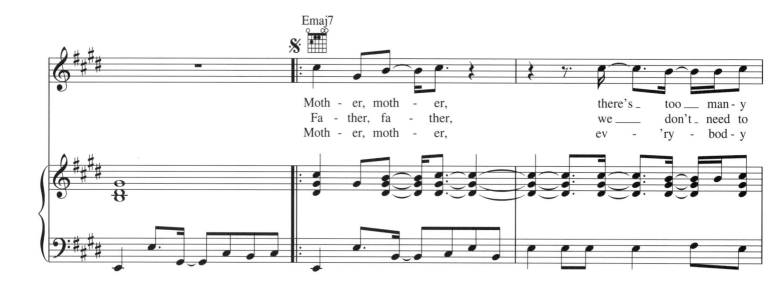

Moth - er, moth - er, there's too man - y
Fa - ther, fa - ther, we don't need to
Moth - er, moth - er, ev - 'ry - bod - y

of you cry - ing.
es - ca - late. Broth - er, broth - er, broth - er,
thinks we're wrong. You see, war is not the an - swer,
Ah, but who are they to judge us

WHEN I NEED YOU

Moderately, with feeling

Words by CAROLE BAYER SAGER
Music by ALBERT HAMMOND

YOU ARE THE SUNSHINE OF MY LIFE

Words and Music by
STEVIE WONDER

YESTERDAY ONCE MORE

Words and Music by JOHN BETTIS
and RICHARD CARPENTER

Moderate Ballad

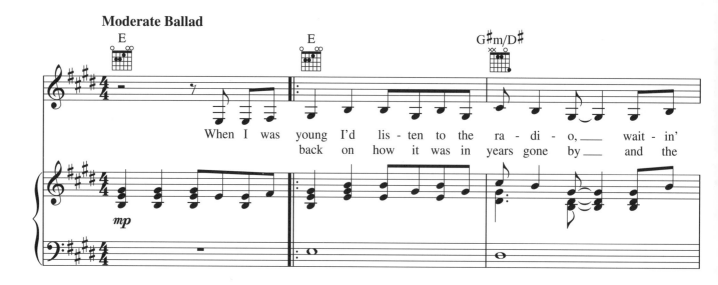

When I was young I'd lis-ten to the ra-di-o,___ wait-in'
back on how it was in years gone by ___ and the

for my fa-v'rite songs.___ When they played, I'd sing a-long;___
good times that I had,___ makes to-day seem rath-er sad;___

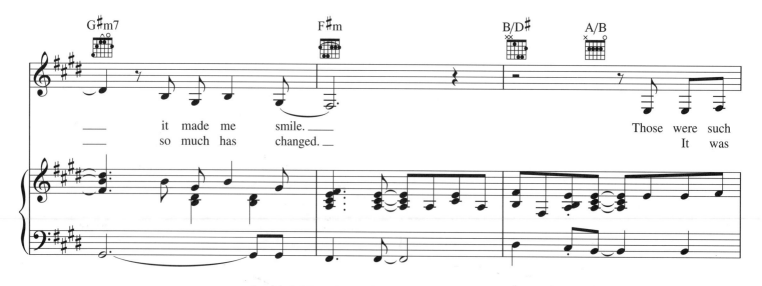

___ it made me smile.___ Those were such
___ so much has changed.___ It was

YOU LIGHT UP MY LIFE

Words and Music by
JOSEPH BROOKS

Moderately slow

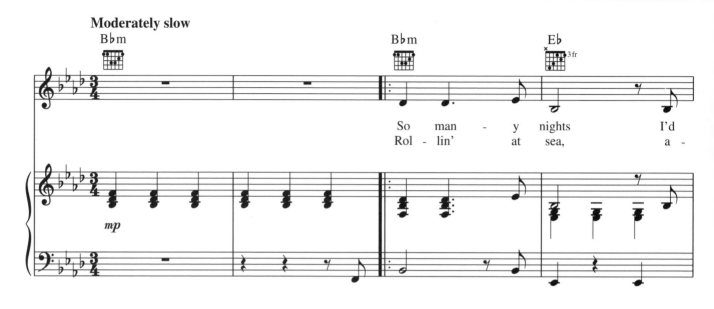

So man - y nights I'd
Rol - lin' at sea, a-

sit by my win - dow wait - ing for some - one ___ to
drift on the wa - ters, could it be fi - n'lly ___ I'm

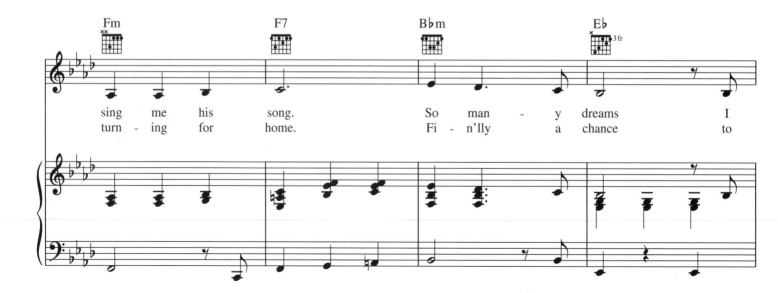

sing me his song. So man - y dreams I
turn - ing for home. Fi - n'lly a chance to

YOU'VE GOT A FRIEND

Words and Music by
CAROLE KING

*Vocal harmony sung 2nd time only

YOUR SONG

Words and Music by ELTON JOHN
and BERNIE TAUPIN

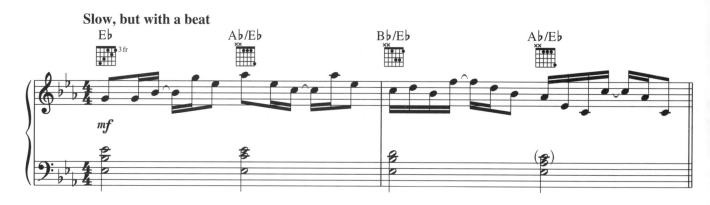

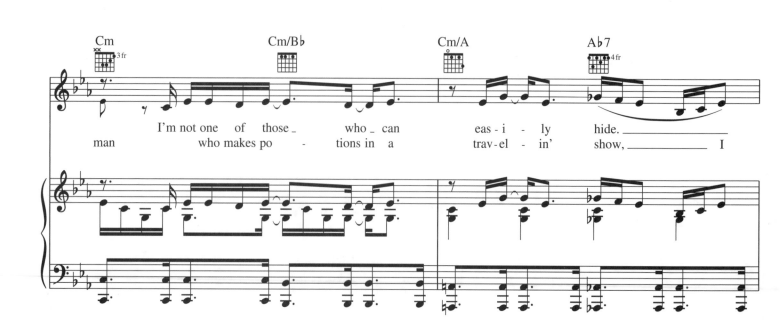

YOU'RE SO VAIN

Words and Music by
CARLY SIMON